Griffin Publishing Group and Teacher Created Materials wish to thank the many talented and devoted supporters of the Olympic Games that made this publication possible.

DIRECTOR OF OPERATIONS	Robin L. Howland	EDITOR	Eric Migliaccio
PROJECT MANAGER	Bryan K. Howland	WRITER	Michelle Breyer
COVER DESIGN	Barb Lorseyedi	ILLUSTRATOR	Howard Chaney

USOC Officers (2001-2004)

Sandra (Sandy) Baldwin, Chair/President
Paul E. George, Vice Chair
Marty Mankamyer, Secretary

Herman R. Frazier, Vice Chair
Brig. Gen. James (Jim) R. Joy (ret.), Vice Chair
Frank Marshall, Treasurer

USOC Management Staff

Scott Blackmun, Acting Chief Executive Officer
Matt Mannelly, Sr. Managing Director, Marketing
Mike Moran, Managing Director, Media Relations & Programs

10 9 8 7 6 5 4 3 2 1

ISBN 1-58000-082-7

Griffin Publishing Group
2908 Oregon Court, Suite I-5, Torrance, CA 90503
Phone (310) 381-0485
www.griffinpublishing.com
Manufactured in the United States of America

Published in association with and distributed by

Teacher Created Materials
6421 Industry Way
Westminster, CA 92683
www.teachercreated.com

Table of Contents

Table of Contents *(cont.)*

Introduction

This book is filled with a variety of puzzles and brain teasers related to the Olympic Games. Each page can be used alone as a quick and easy filler activity or as part of a larger Olympic unit. The pages can be distributed to students as individual worksheets or as small group work. The activities are especially useful in helping students develop:

- logic and other critical thinking skills
- creative thinking skills
- research skills
- spelling skills

- general vocabulary skills
- general knowledge skills
- spatial skills

Several different topics have been provided and repeated throughout the book so that teachers may use a word search, crossword puzzle, and/or brain teaser to reinforce a particular Olympic subject. Depending on the ages and skill levels of your students, you may want to provide lists of crossword puzzle and brain teaser answers to simplify the solving process.

Places to Play

The summer and winter Olympic Games are played at a variety of different locations. Find the many places below in this puzzle.

```
M   O   J   L   G   F   P   O   O   L   L
P   A   R   E   N   A   S   Q   R   B
D   N   H   K   R   E   D   M   C   A
L   I   V   I   T   W   U   Z   E   X
E   B   N   A   M   I   C   T   S   R
I   G   H   G   D   A   R   Y   R   I
F   J   I   A   Y   A   T   D   U   N
K   L   T   M   C   M   E   F   O   K
N   S   G   K   T   R   U   O   C   P
L   A   N   E   O   E   P   O   L   S
```

arena   gym   rink

course   lane   slope

court   mat   stadium

field   pool   track

              ring

The Ancient Games

The Olympic Games originated in Ancient Greece almost 3,000 years ago. Find the words in the puzzle below that relate to this ancient tradition.

```
H   B   N   A   I   M   Y   L   O   D
O   C   F   A   G   H   A   J   K   C
N   P   O   N   T   V   M   A   L   H
O   G   S   O   I   I   W   I   S   A
R   R   E   T   P   A   O   U   P   R
Q   E   S   V   R   E   C   N   I   I
R   E   T   D   W   S   R   Z   R   O
F   C   X   A   I   B   C   A   I   T
Z   E   Y   D   S   U   E   Z   T   D
T   R   A   D   I   T   I   O   N   E
```

award	festival	spirit
chariot	Greece	tradition
cooperate	honor	Zeus
discus	nation	

5

Opening Ceremonies

Each Olympic festival begins with an official ceremony to introduce the athletes and their countries. Find the words in the puzzle below that describe aspects of this ceremony.

```
P  R  E  G  A  L  L  I  V  N
C  E  R  E  M  O  N  Y  O  E
O  S  T  A  E  S  B  I  Q  A
U  D  E  F  G  C  S  U  T  H
N  F  L  A  G  S  I  H  T  C
T  L  E  A  E  P  J  A  O  R
R  N  M  C  M  K  O  M  C  O
Y  E  O  E  A  O  A  X  Y  T
S  R  N  A  R  E  N  A  O  V
P  T  P  R  T  W  P  Q  B  S
```

arena	flags	seats
boycott	games	team
ceremony	oath	torch
country	peace	village
equipment	procession	

Winter Equipment

Winter Olympic athletes use equipment for their competitions. Find these words in the puzzle.

```
E  M  N  S  E  T  A  K  S  M
B  L  S  T  O  N  E  C  O  E
S  O  F  T  I  U  S  O  D  S
C  E  O  I  W  Y  R  A  E  S
C  I  V  T  R  B  L  L  V  T
S  S  J  O  S  B  G  S  D  I
I  E  J  E  L  G  L  M  D  C
K  K  L  Q  O  G  V  R  E  K
S  O  E  G  P  U  C  K  L  Y
P  H  E  L  M  E  T  D  S  V
```

blade	helmet	skis
boots	poles	sled
broom	puck	stick
gloves	rifle	stone
goggles	skates	suit

7

Summer Equipment

Olympic athletes for summer events use many different kinds of equipment. Find the words in the puzzle below.

```
G  A  C  R  A  C  Q  U  E  T
B  T  R  A  N  N  Z  X  N  B
J  P  H  R  P  E  F  U  A  S
T  E  X  E  O  G  G  L  G  E
E  E  R  Y  A  W  L  O  O  O
L  L  R  Y  G  D  G  R  O  H
G  D  H  S  B  G  G  B  A  S
N  D  L  O  L  V  O  E  A  O
I  A  W  E  K  U  Y  C  A  T
S  P  S  K  E  V  O  L  G  R
```

arrow	glove	paddle
ball	goggles	racquet
bat	gun	shoes
bow	headgear	singlet
cap	oar	

Winter Games

Find the 11 sports hidden in the Olympic Winter Games word search below.

```
F  I  G  U  R  E  S  K  A  T  I  N  G
T  S  N  I  C  E  H  O  C  K  E  Y  L
I  P  I  H  O  B  K  E  J  M  G  V  S
M  E  I  W  N  K  P  L  F  X  N  C  N
P  E  K  T  B  K  O  U  V  C  I  O  O
X  D  S  X  M  E  Q  G  P  D  L  W  W
E  S  E  O  B  S  L  E  D  H  R  U  B
R  K  N  T  O  H  L  T  T  P  U  E  O
J  A  I  H  B  E  J  A  W  V  C  I  A
O  T  P  V  S  R  I  M  L  T  V  T  R
B  I  L  D  L  B  R  U  C  O  M  T  D
G  N  A  T  E  B  D  U  R  H  M  T  I
D  G  I  U  D  K  B  K  Y  M  D  K  N
R  W  E  S  K  I  J  U  M  P  I  N  G
```

alpine skiing	figure skating	slalom
biathlon	ice hockey	snowboarding
bobsled	luge	speed skating
curling	ski jumping	

9

Make a Splash

Some of the most popular and successful summer events for the U.S.A. have taken place in the pool. Find the related words in the puzzle below.

```
B  E  V  I  D  C  D  F  I  K  J  S
M  U  L  O  L  O  P  R  E  T  A  W
E  N  T  P  G  R  E  S  E  T  P  I
L  X  O  T  B  A  W  K  V  L  U  M
Y  A  L  B  E  H  I  C  A  A  D  M
T  M  A  Q  Y  R  G  T  Z  Y  H  E
S  N  N  L  K  O  F  J  I  O  G  R
E  Q  E  P  G  O  U  L  A  U  B  E
E  R  O  G  R  T  Y  Z  Y  T  C  F
R  S  L  M  N  O  F  E  K  I  P  D
F  E  K  O  R  T  S  K  C  A  B  J
S  V  L  K  W  X  R  E  L  A  Y  M
```

backstroke   goggles   platform

butterfly   lane   relay

dive   layout   swimmer

freestyle   pike   water polo

One-on-One Competition

Some Olympic athletes perform their skills against opponents. Find the 13 words hidden in the puzzle below relating to martial arts, boxing, wrestling, and fencing.

```
K  D  G  N  I  C  N  E  F  B  T  A
C  N  E  G  K  J  U  D  O  A  H  M
H  B  O  U  T  F  L  O  E  N  G  R
J  I  M  C  R  S  P  K  R  Q  I  Y
G  V  A  U  K  T  W  E  X  N  E  Z
N  G  T  F  E  O  L  W  G  M  W  B
I  H  C  J  N  T  U  D  A  C  Y  A
X  K  H  D  S  L  I  T  M  N  V  O
O  H  O  E  Z  F  A  Y  Q  P  A  R
B  I  R  G  F  O  B  X  U  T  E  S
J  W  M  N  E  I  V  W  C  D  H  O
K  S  L  Q  G  L  O  V  E  S  P  R
```

bout

boxing

fencing

foil

gloves

heavyweight

judo

knockout

mat

match

ring

taekwondo

wrestler

Target Games

Find these summer sports words that involve precision and accuracy. Do you know which sports they describe?

```
S  B  Y  R  E  H  C  R  A  F  G  T
D  N  C  B  I  A  T  H  L  O  N  R
Y  E  O  L  S  Q  S  K  E  E  T  A
C  R  T  E  G  R  A  T  Y  I  H  P
A  T  S  U  G  P  O  E  J  K  F  M
R  B  H  A  V  I  S  N  L  F  I  E
U  X  O  W  C  L  P  E  H  H  R  G
C  E  O  D  L  Z  L  Y  I  C  E  D
C  F  T  U  Y  F  G  J  A  I  M  I
A  Y  B  Z  I  O  Q  S  T  L  B  A
E  T  A  R  T  N  E  C  N  O  C  J
A  X  W  N  P  M  R  L  U  K  E  V
```

accuracy	bullseye	shoot
aim	clay pigeons	skeet
archery	concentrate	target
biathlon	fire	trap
	rifle	

Gymnastics

Hidden in this puzzle are 12 words about gymnastics. See how many you can find.

```
B   S   G   N   I   R   C   E   G   H   M   P
A   L   E   O   T   A   R   D   F   A   I   O
H   V   T   R   O   N   S   Q   E   J   P   M
C   U   N   E   V   E   N   B   A   R   S   M
A   W   Y   Z   M   L   E   K   I   A   J   E
O   S   E   S   I   C   R   E   X   E   K   L
C   U   Y   N   N   X   T   R   T   S   R   H
V   X   B   A   O   Q   A   M   B   O   L   O
C   W   L   P   M   E   M   C   O   D   E   R
P   A   R   A   L   L   E   L   B   A   R   S
B   D   E   Z   G   I   F   H   G   F   H   E
L   T   O   M   K   T   L   U   A   V   J   I
```

balance beam	leotard	rings
coach	mat	team
exercises	parallel bars	uneven bars
floor	pommel horse	vault

Hit! Kick! Dunk!

Below are words relating to summer sports events in which athletes hit, kick, or dunk an object to score points.

K	N	O	T	N	I	M	D	A	B	C	D
E	C	F	H	G	T	E	N	N	I	S	L
K	J	I	T	R	U	O	C	I	H	L	L
R	B	N	T	O	P	R	S	U	A	T	A
Y	A	M	L	S	W	V	T	B	T	E	B
K	T	Q	X	Z	Y	T	T	Q	E	U	E
C	G	E	U	F	L	E	D	C	N	Q	S
U	I	H	J	E	K	L	K	M	N	C	A
P	Y	A	C	S	T	X	V	C	R	A	B
Z	G	O	A	L	B	W	E	U	O	R	T
C	C	B	H	S	O	C	C	E	R	H	G
K	D	I	J	F	D	L	E	I	F	K	L

badminton

baseball

basketball

bat

court

field

goal

hockey stick

net

puck

racquet

shuttlecock

soccer

tennis

Summertime

Almost 40 different types of Olympic sporting events are held during the summer. In the puzzle below are 15 of the lesser known, yet equally challenging, summer events.

A	F	B	D	L	L	A	B	D	N	A	H
S	I	N	N	E	T	E	L	B	A	T	G
C	E	A	R	C	H	E	R	Y	I	F	N
O	L	E	K	L	I	S	H	G	R	O	I
L	D	F	J	M	T	N	O	G	T	P	L
O	H	Q	E	O	N	A	C	N	S	K	I
P	O	R	H	N	S	Y	I	I	E	A	A
R	C	S	V	Z	C	M	U	W	U	Y	S
E	K	W	F	L	D	I	X	O	Q	A	T
T	E	G	I	A	Y	E	N	R	E	K	A
A	Y	N	B	O	X	I	N	G	B	C	D
W	G	H	O	D	N	O	W	K	E	A	T

archery	equestrian	rowing
badminton	fencing	sailing
boxing	field hockey	table tennis
canoe	handball	taekwondo
cycling	kayak	water polo

Olympic Victory

Winning a medal at the Olympics is a great honor for any athlete. Find the words below that describe an Olympic victory.

```
D  E  G  S  E  T  E  L  H  T  A  I
B  C  B  R  O  N  Z  E  C  J  H  L
S  R  O  T  A  T  C  E  P  S  K  N
Q  W  C  M  P  O  R  A  M  V  S  R
M  I  R  F  P  E  S  G  I  C  E  C
R  N  X  V  M  E  T  C  O  V  U  H
O  W  G  O  A  L  T  R  L  L  A  A
F  A  N  Z  P  O  E  I  Y  N  D  M
R  Y  C  R  R  D  S  I  T  H  F  P
E  B  I  Y  E  K  J  H  G  I  N  I
P  D  O  L  A  D  E  M  T  M  O  O
E  P  R  Q  L  M  S  V  U  W  X  N
```

anthem	fan	score
athletes	goal	silver
bronze	gold	spectators
ceremony	medal	victory
champion	perform	win
competition	pride	

Skiing and Snowboarding

Find 16 words in the puzzle below that relate to popular winter sports on a snowy mountain.

A	B	E	D	F	I	E	N	I	P	L	A
D	I	C	H	A	L	F	P	I	P	E	G
R	N	J	S	L	A	I	R	E	A	H	D
A	D	S	E	T	A	G	M	K	P	O	S
O	I	N	C	L	D	W	U	L	W	O	L
B	N	W	N	N	Y	Q	A	N	R	U	A
W	G	X	A	V	P	T	H	X	G	S	L
O	S	H	R	M	U	I	S	O	T	Y	O
N	J	I	U	H	L	G	M	E	Z	A	M
S	K	J	D	L	Q	E	F	C	E	B	D
Y	R	T	N	U	O	C	S	S	O	R	C
N	O	L	E	P	M	S	L	O	P	E	F

aerials	endurance	mogul
alpine	freestyle	slalom
bindings	gates	slope
cross country	half pipe	snowboard
downhill	hand grip	wax
	jump	

17

Olympic Skating

Ice skating is one of the most popular winter events. See how many words you can find that describe the various types of Olympic ice skating.

```
C  F  I  G  U  R  E  O  U  S  N  I  P  S
D  O  E  C  G  F  M  Q  C  S  V  Z  Y  A
I  O  H  Y  E  L  U  I  R  T  W  H  X  C
J  T  A  R  B  D  S  R  I  A  P  U  B  F
N  W  K  O  H  U  A  G  D  A  Y  M  E  P
P  O  I  S  M  J  D  N  R  K  O  K  L  N
N  R  T  L  W  E  A  G  C  S  N  Q  E  R
O  K  V  U  E  B  O  C  D  I  O  C  U  P
S  Y  Z  P  G  E  F  E  R  H  N  I  O  Q
I  J  S  M  R  Y  Z  X  T  A  S  G  N  S
N  L  K  O  S  T  F  I  L  O  R  J  U  K
U  D  H  C  X  G  I  A  N  W  K  E  V  I
S  C  O  R  E  H  B  M  P  L  M  T  Q  L
A  E  C  B  F  S  E  L  G  N  I  S  R  L
```

balance	ice dancing	singles
choreography	lifts	skill
compulsory	music	speed
footwork	pairs	spins
figure	rink	unison
	score	

Running Track

There are many different running events during the Olympics. See how many words you can find in the puzzle below that relate to this summer sport.

```
T  S  E  L  D  R  U  H  A  G  D  F  O  N
O  K  J  E  H  E  N  O  T  A  B  P  E  B
T  I  E  L  S  M  C  B  Q  U  E  S  T  S
H  P  D  A  B  T  N  O  H  T  A  R  A  M
S  E  C  G  R  S  A  B  S  H  E  N  T  R
A  U  T  F  E  A  D  R  C  Q  O  S  E  A
D  I  S  T  A  N  C  E  T  P  C  N  B  S
E  F  C  I  W  G  L  E  R  E  N  H  I  P
V  E  L  N  X  P  O  N  W  U  R  J  K  R
D  P  E  G  E  N  D  U  R  A  N  C  E  I
L  O  A  E  I  K  E  O  N  E  L  M  L  N
A  T  T  G  K  C  A  R  T  A  S  K  F  T
Y  S  S  B  I  D  F  E  N  I  N  G  H  E
S  M  Q  U  C  N  M  E  T  E  R  S  T  R
```

baton	hurdles	speed
cleats	lane	sprinter
dash	marathon	starter
distance	meters	steeplechase
endurance	racewalk	track
	runner	

19

Field Events

Running, jumping, and throwing are the basic skills needed for every sport ever devised. See how many words you can find from the Olympic field events.

```
B  T  T  L  E  R  D  I  S  T  A  N  C  E
A  S  H  O  T  P  U  T  F  E  O  C  L  A
W  I  C  U  R  I  N  G  A  L  D  L  B  R
O  N  P  R  U  D  D  E  H  S  A  L  E  E
R  P  O  Q  A  E  R  T  L  B  G  F  L  M
H  M  H  E  P  T  A  T  H  L  O  N  O  M
T  U  I  N  E  C  C  S  H  L  I  J  N  A
F  J  N  H  E  N  G  H  O  L  K  M  G  H
G  E  E  D  R  N  N  I  L  E  V  A  J  R
O  L  D  K  I  G  H  T  P  I  O  Q  U  S
L  P  M  U  J  H  G  I  H  T  N  E  M  Y
E  I  V  P  L  E  U  T  C  H  A  E  P  Z
X  R  Z  Y  B  D  I  S  C  U  S  G  D  H
W  T  L  U  A  V  E  L  O  P  F  C  I  J
```

ball	heptathlon	scratch line
decathlon	high jump	shot put
discus	javelin	throw
distance	long jump	triple jump
hammer	pole vault	

20

Take Control

Find the words below that relate to summer and winter Olympic sporting events that involve riding, driving, or steering an object to win a medal. Can you guess the different sports?

```
A  V  I  N  E  B  O  B  S  L  E  D  O  M
P  E  S  A  H  C  E  L  P  E  E  T  S  O
D  L  R  S  I  N  G  N  E  S  O  T  G  M
Y  O  A  O  A  K  E  L  E  L  R  N  O  E
N  D  T  S  D  O  C  G  E  E  I  B  A  N
A  R  G  C  P  Y  U  V  A  L  S  F  G  T
M  O  N  A  C  A  N  M  S  T  N  A  N  U
S  M  I  I  T  E  L  A  A  A  L  C  I  M
I  E  B  E  S  I  O  C  M  C  E  H  T  A
S  N  K  R  N  N  L  E  S  I  S  U  F  B
S  A  O  E  I  E  K  U  K  H  C  T  A  I
A  H  D  S  S  A  L  E  G  O  R  E  R  N
H  T  E  E  R  B  S  T  N  E  T  S  D  G
C  A  S  B  F  L  R  E  E  T  S  A  N  S
```

aerodynamic

bicycle

bobsled

brakeman

chassis

chutes

drafting

horse

laps

luge

momentum

obstacles

streamlined

steeplechase

steer

velodrome

Team Sports

There are 15 different Olympic sports listed below that require a team effort. See how many you can find in the puzzle.

```
A B A D M I N T O N A C K S
L L A B T E K S A B K H W T
N G L N V O L L E Y B A L L
S T I A O S A I T A T Y C H
E C O C B F O G L E E T S D
C U B R E T I C R K H I A E
A R H A Y H F P C I G N I L
R L C A L G O O J E Y G L S
Y I K K N L H C S T R A I B
A N Y I O D S P K G B F N O
L G W N L Q B A L E S A G B
E O S E P U P A S T Y S L K
R F I N G E H A L P I N G L
J F K I J S B F G L Q U E N
```

badminton

baseball

basketball

bobsled

curling

field hockey

handball

ice hockey

relay races

rowing

sailing

soccer

softball

volleyball

water polo

Show of Strength

The Olympic sports below involve a combination of strength, concentration, and agility. See if you can find these heavyweight words in the puzzle below.

```
I  N  G  M  U  S  C  L  E  S  E  S  T  R  E  N
C  S  W  U  M  I  E  N  T  U  O  K  C  O  N  K
H  C  R  E  A  R  B  A  L  D  E  R  T  I  G  E
E  M  E  A  I  J  M  G  E  H  E  H  A  R  F  S
A  O  S  V  K  G  A  S  B  D  G  L  E  I  M  T
D  U  T  Y  M  L  H  L  I  I  T  X  K  O  Z  U
S  T  L  M  I  O  K  T  E  A  O  K  W  N  S  O
D  H  E  N  N  V  U  W  L  B  R  N  O  B  Y  B
A  S  R  I  G  E  Y  T  L  I  J  I  N  A  S  O
E  N  H  N  S  V  A  J  H  S  F  Q  D  R  T  U
H  A  T  O  A  E  H  U  A  G  V  T  O  R  R  T
R  T  U  E  H  F  G  D  W  T  U  P  I  I  E  E
E  C  H  A  M  P  I  O  N  O  C  A  K  N  N  L
V  H  N  G  S  H  C  T  A  M  X  H  R  G  G  T
O  I  C  H  T  O  A  M  O  X  E  R  B  D  T  S
N  O  S  L  L  E  B  R  A  B  D  E  C  A  H  P
```

barbells	glove	match	snatch
belt	heavyweight	mouthguard	strength
bouts	judo	muscles	taekwondo
boxer	knockout	overhead	weightlifting
champion	mat	ring	wrestler

Be an Olympian

The Olympics promote the improvement of individuals in mind, body, and spirit. See if you can find words in the puzzle below that describe the characteristics of a true Olympian.

```
A M B A S R O D A S S A B M A R
N E Z C T A L E N T T A O D O R
I D E O R B A S S I B I O N E S
M E D U E F I T R E S P P T W I
A C I R N C A I D C B I A C I E
T N P E G F P I H A R G S L N
S A I G T S K A R S E H Y E L I
O R C A H E M R N P L A O D Z L
S E S R M P L A O L L O J I T P
S V I U I N M O I W G A K N C I
E E D O O S C W S I M Z Y G E C
N S N C T P D M A N S A T S P S
T R U R Q O R S P I R T E H S I
I E O N O I T A N I M R E T E D
F P W G V O S T A M P S O U R I
S X Y R O T I T E P M O C P Q S
```

ambassador	determination	perseverance	strength
champion	discipline	respect	talent
competitor	fair play	spirit	teamwork
cooperate	fitness	sportsmanship	
courage	goodwill	stamina	

Olympic Action Words

Olympic athletes compete in a wide variety of ways. See if you can find the 20 different athletic action words in the puzzle below.

```
G  O  S  W  R  G  S  W  I  N  G  I  N  G  I  R
G  N  F  T  N  O  I  H  G  N  I  C  N  E  F  U
N  I  I  I  R  N  W  B  O  W  L  I  N  L  S  N
G  N  N  L  G  I  N  I  G  O  B  O  I  G  T  I
N  G  D  J  L  G  V  G  N  E  T  P  N  N  G  G
I  A  E  A  B  O  X  I  N  G  P  I  R  I  N  U
P  G  C  C  R  S  R  B  N  I  S  U  N  U  I  N
M  N  T  K  I  C  K  I  N  G  N  G  I  G  N  G
U  I  U  J  I  R  T  G  O  N  N  T  N  G  N  N
J  M  M  S  H  N  I  R  I  I  G  I  G  N  I  I
L  M  B  T  I  N  G  N  H  I  W  T  E  I  W  V
E  I  L  R  G  T  G  C  L  O  I  S  F  T  I  I
A  W  P  O  S  E  T  L  R  G  N  G  I  F  N  D
P  S  N  W  E  I  O  H  I  N  G  I  N  I  G  N
I  I  G  N  P  R  T  G  N  I  P  A  E  L  N  I
N  G  N  I  L  B  M  U  T  N  S  H  O  T  I  N
```

boxing	kicking	rowing	swimming
diving	leaping	running	swinging
fencing	lifting	shooting	throwing
flipping	pitching	sprinting	tumbling
jumping	rolling	striving	winning

Part of the Team

Solve this puzzle by identifying words that relate to the different Olympic team sports.

Across

2. you dunk a basketball through this
6. what a referee blows
7. passed on by relay racers
8. used by a rower
9. another name for birdie
10. person who instructs the team
11. used in tennis and volleyball

Down

1. what you can steal in softball
3. a team sport played in a pool
4. soccer shoes
5. played on ice or a field
6. used in handball
7. in curling, it's used on the ice
8. one who throws strikes

Track Time

Running and jumping are some of the oldest Olympic sports. Solve the puzzle by using track terms.

Across

1. to begin the race
2. an obstacle to clear
3. the 10,000 meter race
5. a longing to win
6. where you end
9. what races are measured in
10. the ability to last
11. races also known as sprints
12. the track is divided into these

Down

1. a short and swift run
4. batons are used in this event
5. different for each type of race
7. where athletes run
8. Track athletes are ranked by their _____.

On the Field

Both track and field events make up the Olympic sport of Athletics. Use your Olympic knowledge to identify these words associated with running, jumping, and throwing.

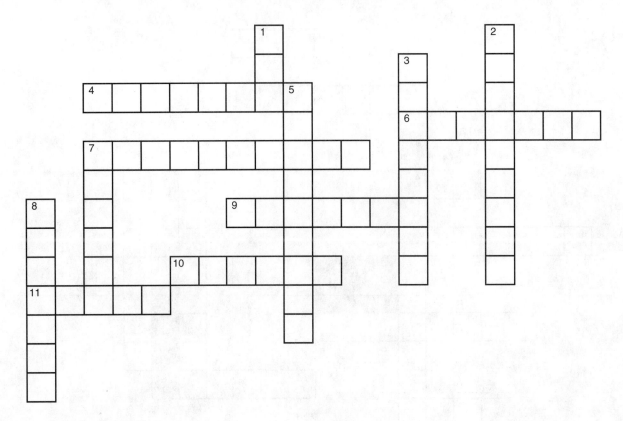

Across

4. to leap over a bar resting between two upright standards
6. the line where a javelin is thrown
7. the women's seven-event sport which replaced the pentathlon in 1984
9. spear that is thrown
10. a steel-rimmed hardwood or metal platter
11. to propel an object forward

Down

1. used to throw the hammer
2. the men's two day, ten-event sport
3. a discus thrower's score is measured by this
5. clearing a crossbar with a long, flexible pole
7. a ball attached to a length of wire that has a metal handle
8. to propel a solid, metal ball through the air as far as possible

Downhill Races

Many Olympic sports use the force of gravity to gain speed downhill. See if you can identify the sports that go with these clues.

Across

2. needed to slow down or stop
5. performed by a single athlete on a sled-like vehicle
6. worn by athletes to cut down friction
10. the capacity for vigorous activity
11. an event using high-speed turns on a heavily snow-bumped slope
12. worn by all downhill racers

Down

1. turned by a mountain biker
2. a team sledding competition
3. both men and _____ compete in alpine skiing
4. a bobsled racetrack
6. alpine and Nordic are two types
7. what a downhill racer hopes to achieve
8. vehicle needed for mountain biking
9. two are used by skiers

Olympic Action

Athletes compete in a variety of ways. Find the athletic action words in this puzzle.

Across

1. leap
3. pitch
6. glide
9. raise
10. opposite of walk
11. opposite of run

Down

2. opposite of pull
3. spin or bend
4. plunge
5. _____ or swim
7. work to achieve
8. opposite of lose

Winter Equipment Crossword

Solve this puzzle by identifying the many kinds of equipment used in the winter Olympics.

Across

2. footwear for snow racing and jumping
4. metal part of an ice skate
7. used to sweep the ice in curling
8. eye protection
10. curling _____
12. shoes for ice
13. object hit in a hockey game

Down

1. long gun
3. head covering
5. ski sticks
6. warm foot coverings
9. hand covering
10. luge or bob_____
11. used to hit a puck

Summer Equipment Crossword

Solve this puzzle by identifying the many kinds of equipment used in the summer Olympics.

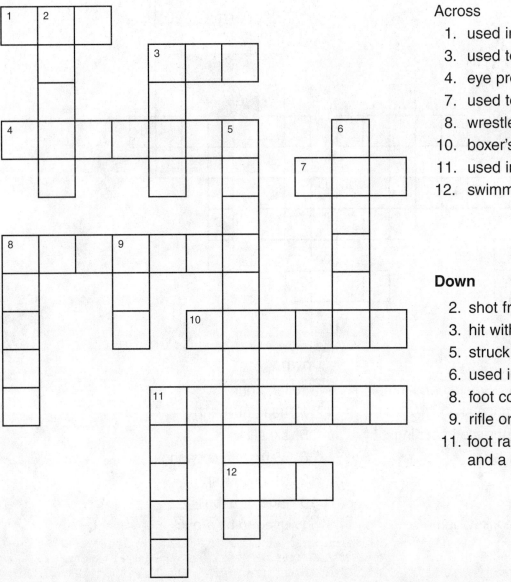

Across

1. used in rowing
3. used to shoot an arrow
4. eye protection
7. used to hit a baseball
8. wrestler's outfit
10. boxer's hand coverings
11. used in tennis
12. swimmer headgear

Down

2. shot from a bow
3. hit with a bat
5. struck in badminton
6. used in table tennis
8. foot covering
9. rifle or pistol
11. foot race with teammates and a baton

Gymnastics

The following puzzle uses words from the exciting sport of gymnastics.

Across

3. men compete on two even _____ bars
4. used on hands to reduce slipping
9. women compete on this raised, 5-meter long board
10. tumble
12. athletes need this to propel themselves through the air

Down

1. leaped over by both men and women
2. a perfect score
3. a leather-covered apparatus with two wooden handles used in the men's competition
4. maneuvers used during the floor exercises
5. the team's instructor
6. routine performed on a 12-meter square mat
7. bars used in the women's competition
8. the famous "iron _____" is performed on rings
11. floor covering

Competitive Swimming

Swimming attracts many different fans from around the world. Use your Olympic knowledge to complete the puzzle below.

Across

1. type of race using more than one swimmer
4. swimmers shave to reduce this
6. what swimmers stand on to begin the race
8. A swimmer is _____ if he/she "jumps the gun" more than once.
10. swimming stroke using a frog-leg kick
11. Racers do this to get into the water.
12. worn to protect the eyes
13. race incorporating four competitive strokes

Down

2. Racers must keep to their own _____.
3. Smooth strokes allow swimmers to _____ through the water.
5. a single swimmer medley race
6. the crawl stroke on one's back
7. a variation of the breaststroke in which arms come back above the surface of the water
9. race in which swimmers may choose their stroke, usually preferring the Australian crawl

In the Pool

Besides competitive swimming, the pool is also used in other Olympic sports. See if you can identify the sports that relate to the words in the puzzle below.

Across

3. points earned
5. to move at the same rate and exactly together
8. team water sport using a ball
9. guarded by the goalie
12. a raised, rigid structure where athletes execute their dives
14. number of starting players on a water polo team
15. a dive with no splash is called a ___ entry
16. flexible diving platform

Down

1. also known as a "straight" dive in which the body must not be bent in any fashion
2. a dive in which the thighs are drawn to the chest to help the athlete "flip"
4. the art of arranging movements for synchronized swimmers
6. one who performs a layout
7. used to score goals in water polo
8. the "jack knife" is an example of this type of dive
10. working together to score a goal
11. other person needed for synchronized swimming
13. bathing caps and suits

Strength and Stamina

Athletes must show both strength and stamina to win Olympic medals. Solve this puzzle by using words that describe sports that require these skills.

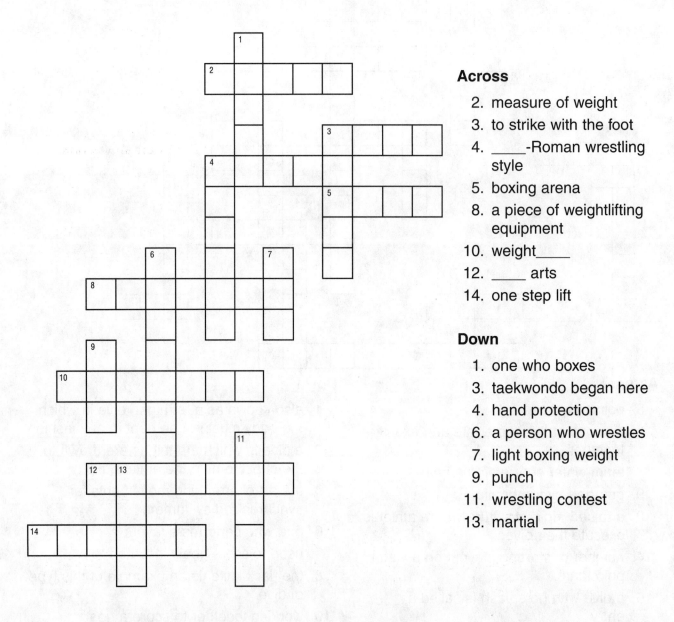

Across

2. measure of weight
3. to strike with the foot
4. ____-Roman wrestling style
5. boxing arena
8. a piece of weightlifting equipment
10. weight____
12. ____ arts
14. one step lift

Down

1. one who boxes
3. taekwondo began here
4. hand protection
6. a person who wrestles
7. light boxing weight
9. punch
11. wrestling contest
13. martial ____

Winter Events

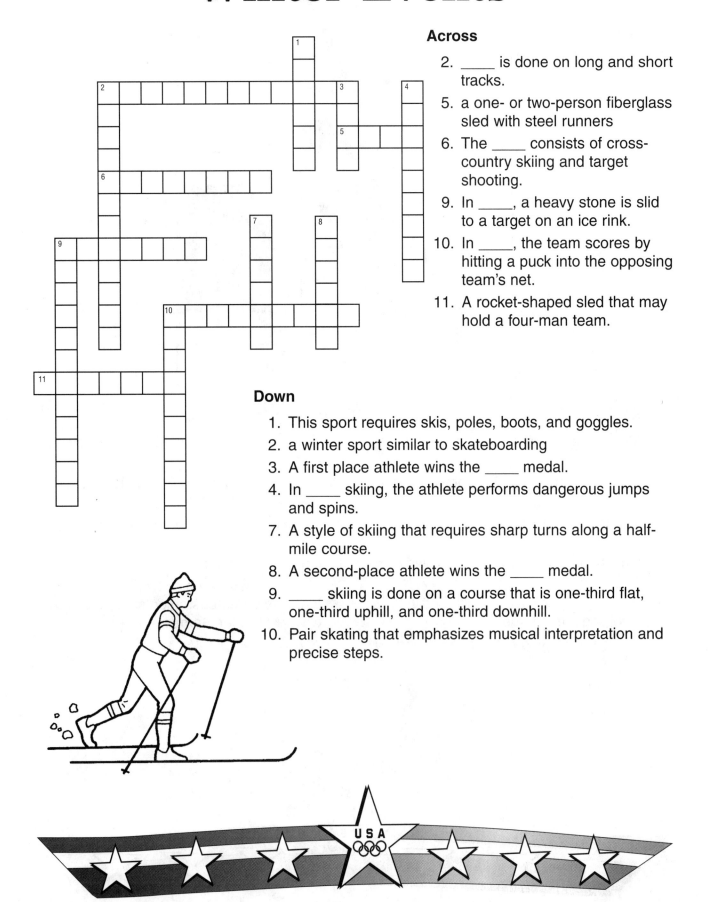

Across

2. _____ is done on long and short tracks.

5. a one- or two-person fiberglass sled with steel runners

6. The _____ consists of cross-country skiing and target shooting.

9. In _____, a heavy stone is slid to a target on an ice rink.

10. In _____, the team scores by hitting a puck into the opposing team's net.

11. A rocket-shaped sled that may hold a four-man team.

Down

1. This sport requires skis, poles, boots, and goggles.

2. a winter sport similar to skateboarding

3. A first place athlete wins the _____ medal.

4. In _____ skiing, the athlete performs dangerous jumps and spins.

7. A style of skiing that requires sharp turns along a half-mile course.

8. A second-place athlete wins the _____ medal.

9. _____ skiing is done on a course that is one-third flat, one-third uphill, and one-third downhill.

10. Pair skating that emphasizes musical interpretation and precise steps.

USA

Winter Sports

Across

2. Most winter sporting events need _____.
4. Each sporting contest is known as an _____.
5. Two skaters together make up a _____.
7. Cross-country skiing is also known as _____.
9. A _____ is a type of ski race involving many turns.
10. _____ skating is a graceful sport.
11. A _____ is a sled that one rides lying on his or her back.
12. _____ is a form of the slalom.

Down

1. The _____ is a combination of skiing and shooting.
2. _____ is a sport for people who are not afraid of heights.
3. If a skier falls, his clothes can get _____.
6. Ice _____ is a sport using a puck.
8. _____ is a team sport played on ice that was a demonstration sport in seven Olympic Winter Games.

The Modern Games

Use the clues below to solve the puzzle about the Modern Olympic Games.

Across

4. third-place medal
5. The Olympics originated in this country.
8. The Games promote world ____.
9. Athletes live here during the Games.
12. city in Greece
14. second place medal
15. The Games promote ____ among athletes.

Down

1. warm-weather Games
2. game
3. used to broadcast the Games
6. 10-event Olympic sport
7. cold-weather Games
10. Olympic participants
11. protest
13. award
16. The Olympic Games last sixteen ____.
17. first place medal

The Ancient Games

Across

5. day three: religious ____
6. valley in ancient Greece
10. two-wheeled, horse-drawn carriage
12. arena
14. five-event competition
15. king of the gods
16. athletes ate this
17. feast

Down

1. They could not attend the Ancient Games.
2. to leap
3. sprint
4. day two: ____ to the gods
5. wreck, head-on ____
7. wife of Zeus
8. toss for distance
9. competitors
11. The Olympic Games is a sports ____ .
13. four-year period

Summer Sports

How many different summer sports can you name? In the puzzle below are just a few. Use the back of this paper to list any others that you may know.

Across

5. most widely played team sport in the world
6. a martial art
7. to try and pin your opponent to a mat
8. often referred to as ping-pong
11. sport trying to achieve a "rip" entry
12. track and field
13. gloves are worn for this sport
15. ice or field ____
16. yachting
17. races on bikes

Down

1. sport incorporating strength and agility on apparatus
2. Olympic competition involving horses
3. you perform a "spike" in _____ball
4. foils are used in this sport
7. to raise heavy barbells overhead
9. needs a shuttlecock and racquet
10. team pool sport
14. one-man enclosed canoe

Hit the Target

Identify these words related to Olympic sports that require an athlete to aim at a target.

Across

1. otherwise known as trap shooting
2. what one aims at
6. Steady nerves and _____ are needed to focus on one's target.
8. weapons that fire
9. sport using a bow and arrow
10. A perfect score is called a bull's _____.
12. shot from a bow
13. _____-country skiing is part of the biathlon.
15. mechanical exactness
16. shoot
18. discharging a weapon
19. used in archery

Down

1. part of a gun used to focus on the target
3. where a shooting competition takes place
4. clay targets or _____ flung into the air
5. type of guns used in rapid fire and free competitions
6. load of ammunition
7. focus on the target
11. pin-point precision
14. combination of cross-country skiing and rifle shooting
17. a shooting competition

Ride It!

Many Olympic sports require an athlete to ride, drive, and steer an object to achieve the fastest time possible. Use the clues below to identify words associated with these sports.

Across

4. having a surface designed to offer the least possible resistance to wind
7. sports arena equipped with a bank track for cycling
12. equestrian obstacle course
14. hedge or other barrier to overcome during a race
16. turns around the track
18. body of the bobsled
19. athlete who slows down the bobsled
20. force or speed of movement

Down

1. method of training a horse in precision of movement
2. team winter sport down a chute
3. type of cycling
5. Bobsled riders sit _____ their sled.
6. riding in the air current created by the leader
8. horse rider
9. drive
10. worn by an athlete to reduce friction
11. mechanics that deal with the motion of air
13. single-athlete sledding sport
15. sport on two wheels
17. where bobsleds are raced

Olympic Spirit

How many of the following characteristics do you share with Olympic athletes?

Across

1. bravery
7. the ability to lift heavy weights
9. Whether you win or lose, you should always use good ____.
13. steadfastness
14. Each athlete is an ambassador of international ____.
15. good physical condition and health
16. country
17. a fixed purpose or intention to succeed

Down

2. to admire or honor
3. slang for winner
4. Training each day requires this.
5. working together towards a goal
6. good sportsmanship or fair ____
7. the ability to endure
8. working together as a team
10. feeling good about yourself, or high ____-esteem
11. better than the rest
12. one who competes

44

The Olympic Experience

The roar of the crowds, the music, and the events are all part of the Olympic experience. Use the clues to solve the puzzle describing what you might encounter at the Olympics.

Across

3. They are displayed to represent the competing countries.
5. the third place medal
7. the Olympic flame
11. what athletes repeat at the opening ceremonies
12. played during the medal ceremony
14. what each athlete brings their country
15. a win
16. desire to succeed
18. first place medal
19. a call to engage in a contest
20. traditional ritual

Down

1. procession
2. group of athletes working together
3. supporters
4. people watching the Olympic events
5. when a country chooses not to attend the Olympics for political or philosophical reasons
6. place to conduct sporting events
8. winner, superior athlete
9. a contest
10. second place medal
13. to execute one's sport
15. community of Olympic athletes
17. during the Olympics, all countries vow to maintain a state of ____

Olympic Stars

Supply the missing names of the American Olympic medalists in the puzzle below.

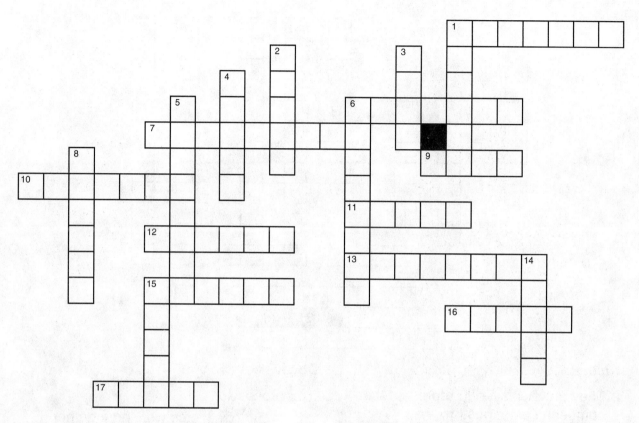

Across

1. basketball player _____ Jordan
6. gymnast _____ Retton
7. figure skater Kristi _____
9. speed skater _____ Heiden
10. boxer Joe _____
11. swimmer Janet _____
12. heptathlete _____ Joyner-Kersee
13. diver Greg _____
15. swimmer Matt _____
16. track and field star Carl _____
17. track star Jesse _____

Down

1. gymnast Shannon _____
2. gymnast Kerri _____
3. figure skate _____ Lipinski
4. speed skater Bonnie _____
5. tennis star Jennifer _____
6. figure skater _____ Kwon
8. speed skater Dan _____
14. swimmer Mark _____
15. wrestler _____ Baumgartner

46

Host Cities

Identify Olympic Games host cities using the clues below. Place each answer in the puzzle. Use the map on page 70 to help with clues.

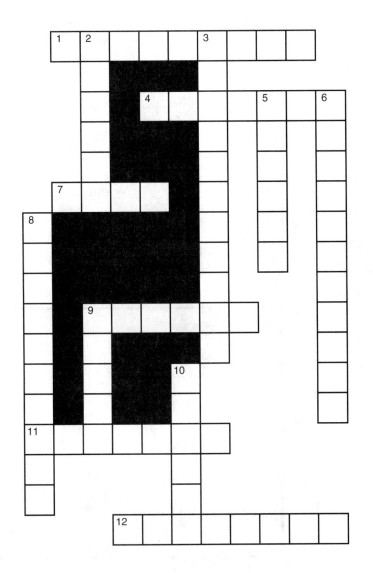

Across

1. _____, Spain (Summer, 1992)

4. _____, Georgia, USA (Summer, 1996)

7. _____, Norway (Winter, 1952)

9. _____ Australia (Summer, 2000)

11. _____, Canada (Winter, 1988)

12. _____, Canada (Summer, 1976)

Down

2. _____, Greece (Summer, 1896 & 2004)

3. _____, Norway (Winter, 1994)

5. _____, Japan (Winter, 1998)

6. _____, France (Winter, 1992)

8. _____, New York, USA (Winter, 1932 & 1980)

9. _____, South Korea (Summer, 1988)

10. _____, Germany (Summer, 1936)

Olympic Competitions

Fill in the missing letters to reveal information and highlights of the Olympic Games in 1932 and 1936. Write the words on the lines below.

1.

_____ road jump

hamm _____ r throw

ma _____ athon

Lutz _____ ong

runn _____ ng

Germa _____ y

2.

Jesse _____ wens

ath _____ etes

victor _____

gold _____ edals

shot _____ ut

Amer _____ cans

de _____ athlon

track _____ tar

3.

pentath _____ on

Calif _____ rnia

di _____ cus

tr _____ ck

boxi _____ g

rowin _____

r _____ lay races

water po _____ o

hurdl _____ s

_____ wimming

4.

long ju _____ p

f _____ ncing

_____ iving

dec _____ thlon

wrest _____ ing

back _____ troke

1. _____

2. _____

3. _____

4. _____

Olympic People and Places

Write the numbers from the clues below next to the matching athletes or countries on the Olympic podium. The first one has been done for you.

		Mary Lou Retton ___	Bonnie Blair _1_		
		Carl Lewis ___	Matt Biondi ___		
Canada ___	Australia ___	Janet Evans ___	Eric Heiden ___	Afghanistan ___	Mexico ___
South Korea ___	Norway ___	Bruce Jenner ___	Greg Louganis ___	Japan ___	United States ___

1. She set a world record in winning 500-meter speed skating.
2. He was the first athlete to win five individual gold medals at one Olympic Games.
3. This country hosted the 2000 summer Olympic Games.
4. This country hosted the 1968 summer Olympic Games.
5. This country hosted the 1980 winter Olympic Games.
6. This country hosted the 1988 winter Olympic Games.
7. This country hosted the 1988 summer Olympic Games.
8. This country hosted the 1994 winter Olympic Games.
9. This country hosted the 1998 winter Olympic Games.
10. This track and field athlete participated in four Olympic Games.
11. This gymnast won the all-around gold medal in the 1984 Olympic Games.
12. She holds records in three freestyle swimming events.
13. This male swimmer won five gold, one silver, and one bronze medal.
14. This decathlete was one of the stars of the 1976 Olympics.
15. He was the first diver to win springboard and platform events in two Olympic Games.

You should have one word left. The remaining word names the country whose invasion by the Soviet Union caused U.S. President Jimmy Carter to ask the Olympic Committee to boycott the 1980 Olympic games in Moscow. This country was _____.

Games in Ancient Greece

To find out more about the Olympic Games held in Ancient Greece, fill in the blanks below. Use the Word Bank to help you find the missing word that completes each sentence.

Word Bank

wrestling	excluded	rod	chariot
five	Olympia	horse	pentathlon
foot	athletes	citizens	gods

1. The early Olympic Games were held in the Valley of _____.

2. All Greek male _____ were invited to attend.

3. Both _____ and judges went early to train for the Games.

4. The first Olympic Games features only one event, a _____ race.

5. During the Games, sacrifices were offered to Zeus, the king of the Greek _____.

6. In time, the Olympic Games became a _____-day festival.

7. The first sporting event of these festival Games was the _____ race.

8. There was also a bareback _____ race.

9. The _____ included five events.

10. In this five-event sport, the final event was _____.

11. Judges carried a _____ to enforce the rules.

12. Women were _____ from the Olympic Games

Sports Analogy Challenge

See if you can solve these analogies for sports of the summer and winter Olympic Games. An analogy is used to compare two ideas. To solve it, think how the first set of words is related. Then fill in the blank with a word that relates in the same manner to the word at the end of the sentence.

1. A ball is to field hockey as a p u c k is to ice hockey.

2. Six is to volleyball as __ __ __ __ is to basketball.

3. Paddle is to canoeing as an __ __ __ is to rowing.

4. Racquet is to tennis as a __ __ __ __ __ __ is to table tennis.

5. A foil is to fencing as a __ __ __ __ __ is to boxing.

6. A vault is to a gymnast as a __ __ __ __ __ __ __ is to a track star.

7. A goal is to soccer as a __ __ __ is to baseball.

8. A ring is to a boxer as a __ __ __ __ is to an ice dancer.

9. A six is to figure skating as a __ __ __ is to gymnastics.

10. An inning is to baseball as a __ __ __ __ __ is to boxing.

11. A bat is to baseball as a __ __ __ __ __ is to ice hockey.

12. A net is to team handball as a __ __ __ __ is to basketball.

13. Sit is to a bobsled as __ __ __ is to a luge.

14. A cleat is to a baseball player as a __ __ __ __ __ is to a skater.

15. Shoot is to an arrow as __ __ __ __ __ is to a javelin.

16. A mat is to a gymnast as a __ __ __ __ __ __ is to a tennis player.

17. A knockdown is to a boxer as a __ __ __ __ is to a wrestler.

18. In skiing, alpine is to slalom as __ __ __ __ __ __ __ is to cross-country.

19. A hand is to water polo as a __ __ __ __ is to soccer.

20. Pentathlon is to five as __ __ __ __ __ __ __ __ __ is to ten.

Famous Olympians

How well do you know the Olympic stars? Match each star below with his or her description in the opposite column.

_____1. Abebe Bikila

_____2. Dawn Fraser

_____3. Jesse Owens

_____4. Olga Korbut

_____5. Eric Heiden

_____6. Cassius Clay

_____7. Eddie Eagan

_____8. Mark Spitz

_____9. Rosi Mittermaier

_____10. Babe Didrikson

_____11. Patricia McCormick

_____12. Daley Thompson

_____13. Sonja Henie

_____14. Jean-Claude Killy

_____15. Bob Mathias

_____16. Dick Button

_____17. Sammy Lee

A. popular woman diver

B. Norway's skating queen

C. barefoot marathon winner

D. became heavyweight champ of the world

E. almost swept the alpine for her country

F. winning Australian swimmer

G. track star of the Berlin Games

H. won seven gold medals in swimming

I. winter and summer medalist

J. sparked interest in gymnastics

K. youngest decathlon winner

L. won diving gold and coached another winner

M. swept alpine events

N. U.S. figure skating champion

O. Won five gold medals in speed skating

P. two-time decathlon winner for Great Britain

Q. great all-around female athlete

Olympic Numbers

Circle the correct number for each question.

1. The first official Olympics occurred in 1948   193 B.C.   776 B.C. . Although the games had been taking place for many years previously, this was the first year in which winners were actually documented.

2. The very first Olympic games consisted of only one event, a footrace 200 yards   180 meters   47 feet long.

3. Still, the first Olympic games drew a crowd of over 70,000   28,000   1,000 spectators.

4. The Olympic games were held in tribute to Zeus, and athletes competed every four   seven   two years.

5. In Olympia, where the games were held, there stood a 12-foot   40-foot   6-foot statue of Zeus made of gold and ivory. It is considered one of the Seven Wonders of the Ancient World.

6. As the Olympics grew more popular, athletes from all over the world came to compete. To qualify, they were required to arrive 1 year   13 days   1 month prior to the games for training.

7. Soon, more and more events were added to the competition. By the 5th century B.C., there were 13   26   9 different events.

8. One of the more exciting events was a chariot race in the Hippodrome, a flat arena with a post at each end. The racers had to make 100   12   51 turns around the posts, which meant they covered about 5 1/2 miles.

9. Another popular event was the pentathlon. The winner was the athlete who completed 2   3   4 of 5   7   9 different events.

10. Although the games were mainly a man's sport, boys from the ages of 6   10   12 to 17 were allowed to compete.

Draw a Famous Olympic Statue

Use the clues below to draw a famous Greek statue using the enlarged grid on the following page.

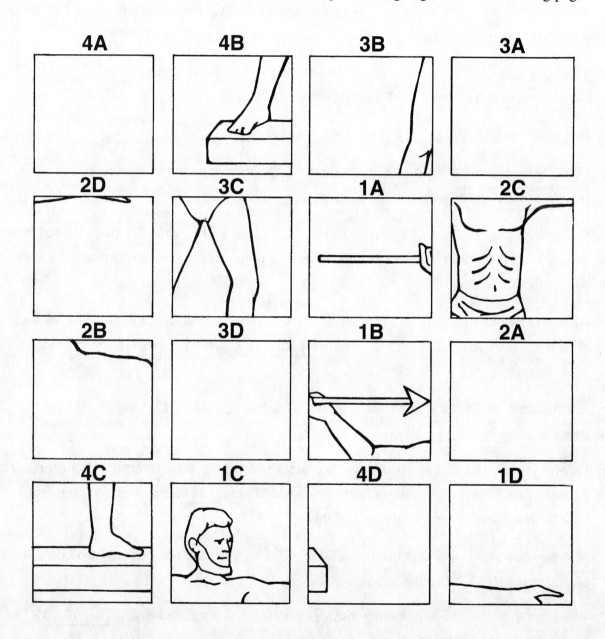

Draw a Famous
Olympic Statue *(cont.)*

	A	B	C	D
1				
2				
3				
4				

Sports Riddles

Read the clues and use the sports from the Word Bank to fill in the blanks. Use the numbered letters to fill in the blanks below and complete the puzzle.

Word Bank

archery	cycling	wrestling
luge	rowing	skating
gymnastics	equestrian	fencing

This sport was used in prehistoric times for hunting. __ __ __ __ __ __ __
                                                      1   9

This freestyle sport was once popular at the ancient Olympian Games.

__ __ __ __ __ __ __ __ __
     2

College teams often compete in this water sport. __ __ __ __ __ __
                                                      3

Men and women perform acrobatic tumbling movements.

__ __ __ __ __ __ __ __ __ __
 4   7

The foil, epee, and saber are used in the sport. __ __ __ __ __ __ __
                                                      5

The slider wears a tight rubber suit and pointed boots. __ __ __ __
                                                              8

Show jumping and dressage are events in this sport.

__ __ __ __ __ __ __ __ __ __
10   6

Riders race in a large group called a peloton. __ __ __ __ __ __ __
                                                      11

Having good blades is important in all events of this sport. __ __ __ __ __ __ __

The site of the first modern Olympic Games:

City: __ __ __ __ __ __   Country: __ __ __ __ __ __
       1 7 9 2 6 12   4 3 10 5 11 8

Decathlon Maze

Training for the decathlon is not easy. Follow the path past each of the events to the medal.

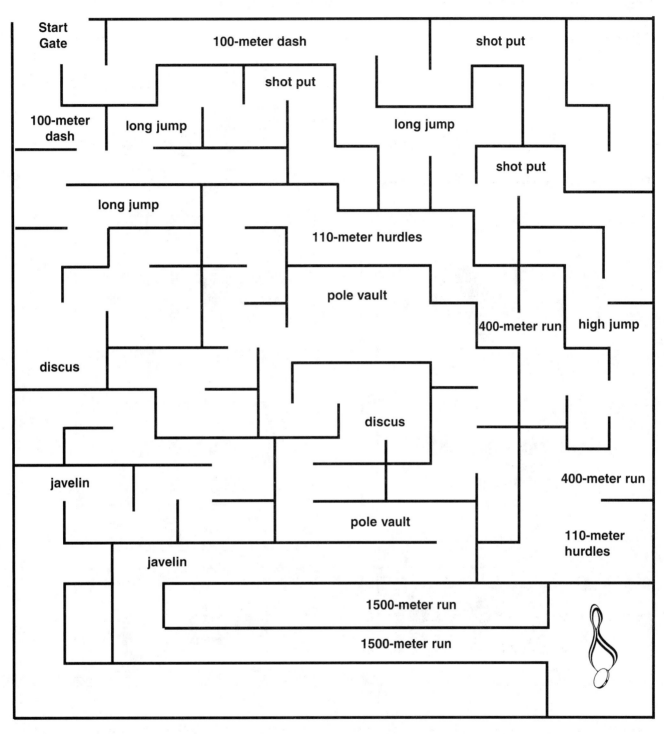

Start Gate

100-meter dash

shot put

shot put

100-meter dash

long jump

long jump

long jump

shot put

110-meter hurdles

pole vault

400-meter run

high jump

discus

discus

400-meter run

javelin

pole vault

110-meter hurdles

javelin

1500-meter run

1500-meter run

USA

License Plates

Car license plates often tell something about their owners. Read each imaginary license plates and name an Olympic athlete who might own each car.

Hint: Adding vowels will help solve the puzzles.

1.  SPDSK8R

_____

2.  GR8 BXR

_____

3.  DRM TM

_____

4.  FGRSK8R

_____

5. N01 DVR

_____

6. SOCRGRT

_____

7. 7GOLD72

_____

8. 10 4GLD

_____

USA

United States Olympians

Read the clues and fill in the last names of these medal winners. The first names are given.

1. 1936 track and field   O _ _ _ _ (Jesse)

2. eight gold medals, track and field   L _ _ _ _ (Carl)

3. 1992 figure-skating gold medalist   Y _ _ _ _ _ _ _ _ _ (Kristi)

4. member, 1992 basketball Dream Team   M _ _ _ _ _ _ (Karl)

5. won seven gold medals, swimming   _ P _ _ _ (Mark)

6. gold-medal figure skater, 1998   _ I _ _ _ _ _ _ (Tara)

7. 1992 gold medalist in tennis   _ A _ _ _ _ _ _ (Jennifer)

8. speed-skating medalist, 1994   _ _ N _ _ _ (Dan)

9. gold-medal gymnast, 1996   S _ _ _ _ (Keri)

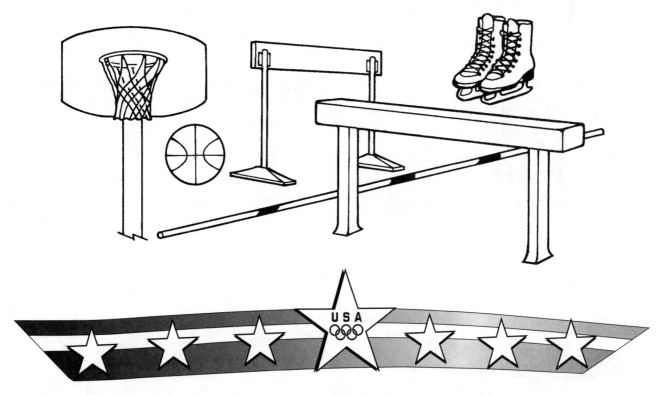

Events and Equipment

Analyze these groups of letters to solve the puzzles. They are in order, no letters have been omitted, but they cannot be read only from left to right. Patterns may be horizontal or vertical. Pay close attention to the clues provided.

1. archery equipment

```
B   A   O   T   G
O   R   W   A   E
W   R   S   R   T
```

_____

_____

2. baseball equipment

```
B   A   L   L
B   A   T   G
L   O   V   E
```

_____

_____

3. two sports that require a net

```
T   E   N   N
O   V   S   I
L   L   E   Y
L   L   A   B
```

_____

_____

4. track and field events

```
U   C   S   I   D
S   J   A   V   E
H   S   N   I   L
O   T   P   U   T
```

_____

_____

5. two gymnastic events

```
P   L   B   A   N   *
A   E   A   L   C   M
R   L   R   A   E   A
A   L   S   B   B   E
```

_____

_____

6. two water sports

```
L   I   E   I
I   N   O   N
A   G   N   G
S   C   A   *
```

_____

_____

7. pentathlon events

```
F   E   N   C   I   N
G   R   I   D   I   N
G   S   H   O   O   T
I   N   G   R   U   N
N   I   N   G   S   W
I   M   M   I   N   G
```

_____

_____

_____

_____

_____

60

Easy Analogies

Determine the relationship between the items and complete these analogies.

1. walk is to _____ as trot is to gallop

2. win is to lose as hit is to _____

3. cold is to winter Olympics as _____ is to summer Olympics

4. fast is to run as slow is to _____

5. gold is to first place as _____ is to second place

6. swimmer is to _____ as sprinter is to track

7. ball is to bat as _____ is to stick

8. teach is to coach as compete is to _____

9. snow is to mountain as _____is to field

10. throw is to arm as _____ is to leg

11. bicycle is to cycling as _____ is to luge

12. vault is to gymnast as _____is to skier

13. grass is to _____ as ice is to hockey

14. sixes are to ice skating as _____ are to gymnastics

More Analogies

To complete an analogy, you must first determine the relationship between the items. For example, the relationship may be athlete to sport, athlete to country, or sport to equipment. You may use a reference book to help you. Analogies are read as follows:

Example: Michael Jordan : basketball :: Jim Abbott : baseball.

Michael Jordan is to basketball as Jim Abbott is to baseball.

1. Paavo Nurmi : Finland :: Jesse Owens : _____

2. Kipchoge Keino : Kenya :: Abebe Bikila : _____

3. Greg Louganis : _____ :: Janet Evans : swimming

4. first place : _____ :: second place : silver

5. bow and arrow : _____ :: ball and glove : baseball

6. bicycle : cycling :: _____ : equestrian

7. kicking : _____ :: hitting : tennis

8. boxing : _____ :: tennis : court

9. second place : silver :: _____ : bronze

10. throw : discus :: _____ : basketball

11. runner : _____ :: wrestler : mat

12. volleyball : hands :: tennis : _____

13. men: parallel bars :: women : _____

14. five events : _____ :: ten events : decathlon

What's Missing?

Look at the pictures of athletic equipment. In each box, draw a piece of equipment that belongs with the others.

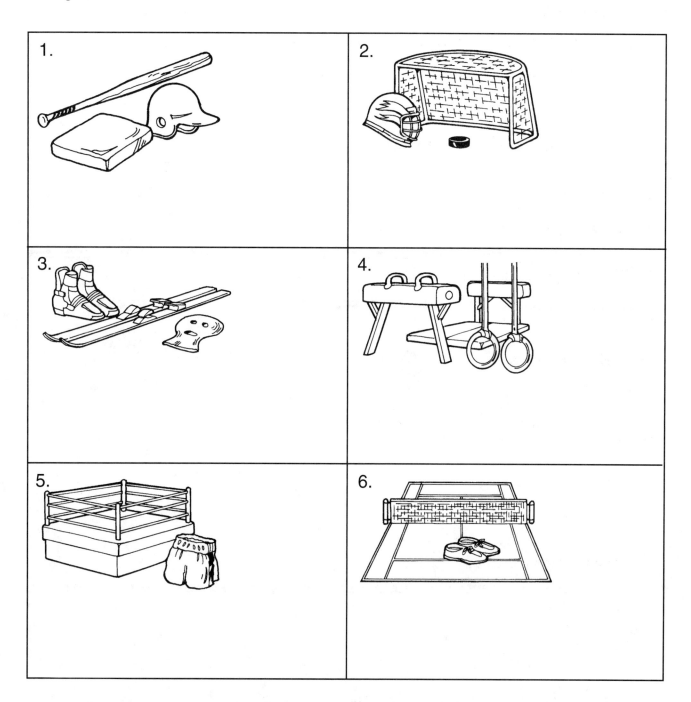

The Olympic Experience

Fill in the missing letters and answer the questions.

T__RCH

S__ORTS

M__DALIST

I__DIVIDUAL

STAD__UM

BRO__ZE

__OLD

__OACH

GR__ECE

SILVE__

EV__NTS

SWIM__ING

SPECTAT__RS

RU__NER

PLA__ERS

The Olympic flame is lit at the _____.

ARCHER__

SOCC__R

WREST__ING

CYC__IST

DECATHL__N

RO__ING

HU__DLES

SILV__R

JU__O

__YMNASTICS

T__ACK

FI__LD

JAV__LIN

TE__NIS

Name the five colors of the rings on the Olympic symbol: blue, black,

_____, _____, and _____.

64

Categories

Read the clues and name each sport. Use the Word Bank to help you.

Word Bank

archery	gymnastics	sledding	hockey
tennis	basketball	swimming	skating
skiing	track and field	baseball	fencing

1. target, arrow, bow— _____

2. hoop, court, ball— _____

3. ball, fielder's glove, bat— _____

4. net, racquet, ball— _____

5. lane, finish line, shoes— _____

6. stick, puck, helmet— _____

7. bout, touche, foil— _____

8. butterfly, pool, crawl— _____

9. poles, boots, jump— _____

10. track, blade, rink— _____

11. goggles, padding, luge— _____

12. vault, uneven bars, rings— _____

Imaginary Web Sites

These imaginary Web sites could lead you to information about famous Olympians. Use an encyclopedia to help you name an athlete closely linked to each of the following sites.

1. www.fgsktng/gold/women.com _____

2. www.fgsktng/gold/men.com _____

3. www.wrestler.org _____

4. www.T&F/discus/men.com _____

5. www.T&F/javelin/women.com _____

6. www.Ttennis.dbls/men.org _____

7. www.cyclesprint.1000m/gold _____

8. www.bttrflyswm/solo.win _____

9. www.SYNswm/duo.win _____

10. www.gym/team/gold.org _____

11. www.skijmpr/men/gold _____

12. www.soccr.women/gold _____

13. www.hoops/gold/1992 _____

14. www.no.1/divr/ _____

15. www.bobsld/team/champs _____

16. www.USspdsktr.com/5gold _____

17. www.worldrecord.com/200M/19.32 _____

18. www.UShockey.com/1980/heroes _____

Headlines

Analyze the code to find the answers. The years will help you name the athletes.

1	2	3	4	5	6	7	8	9	10	11	12	13	14	15	16	17	18	19	20	21	22	23	24	25	26
A	B	C	D	E	F	G	H	I	J	K	L	M	N	O	P	Q	R	S	T	U	V	W	X	Y	Z

1. (1998)

21-19   6-5-13-1-12-5   23-9-14-19   19-11-1-20-9-14-7   7-15-12-4

_____   _____   _____   _____   _____

_____   _____ (athlete's name)

2. (1936)

2-5-18-12-9-14   8-15-14-15-18-19   21-19   20-18-1-3-11   19-20-1-18

_____   _____   _____   _____   _____

_____   _____ (athlete's name)

3. (1948)

21-19   13-1-14   25-15-21-14-7-5-19-20   4-5-3-1-20-8-12-15-14   23-9-14-14-5-18

_____   _____   _____   _____   _____

_____   _____ (athlete's name)

4. (1972)

21-19   19-23-9-13-13-5-18   20-1-11-5-19   19-5-22-5-14   7-15-12-4-19

_____   _____   _____   _____   _____

_____   _____ (athlete's name)

5. (1996)

23-9-14-14-9-14-7   7-25-13-14-1-19-20   9-14-10-21-18-5-19   1-14-11-12-5

_____   _____   _____   _____

_____   _____ (athlete's name)

Athlete Picture Clues

Use these picture clues to identify famous International Olympians. Choose from the Athlete Box.

Athlete Box

A. Sonja Henie   **D.** Abebe Bikila

B. Dawn Fraser   **E.** Anton Sailer

C. Paavo Nurmi   **F.** Nadia Comaneci

1. _____

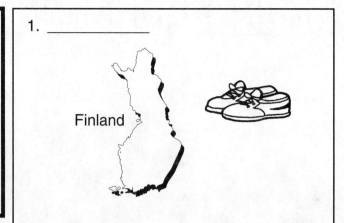

2. _____

3. _____

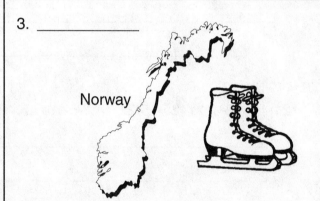

4. _____

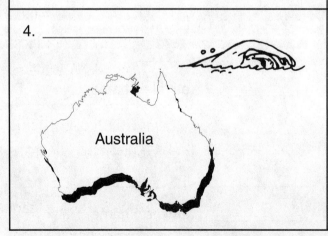

5. _____

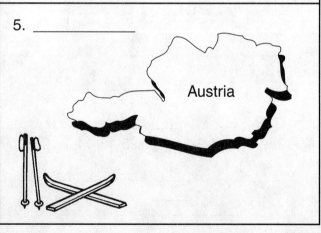

Olympic Dream Teams

Fill in the blanks and fit the answers into the puzzle. Use the Word Bank to help you.

Word Bank

hockey	gold	gymnast
coach	talent	women's
world	boxing	basketball

1. Jesse Owens won four _____ medals at the 1936 Berlin Games.

2. The U.S. _____ team beat Finland at Lake Placid.

3. Several members of the 1976 U.S. _____ team became professional athletes.

4. The winning teams are the best in the _____.

5. The 1960 U.S. _____ team beat Brazil in Rome.

6. The Soviet Union had the world's best _____ gymnastics team in 1976.

7. Athletes who excel at their sports have natural _____.

8. Pat Nappi was the _____ of the 1976 U.S. Boxing team.

9. Nelli Kim was a _____ on the 1976 Soviet Union women's team.

Name the City

Identify the Olympic cities on the map below. Use encyclopedias or reference books to help you. Write the name of the city on the corresponding line on page 47 and fill in the crossword puzzle.

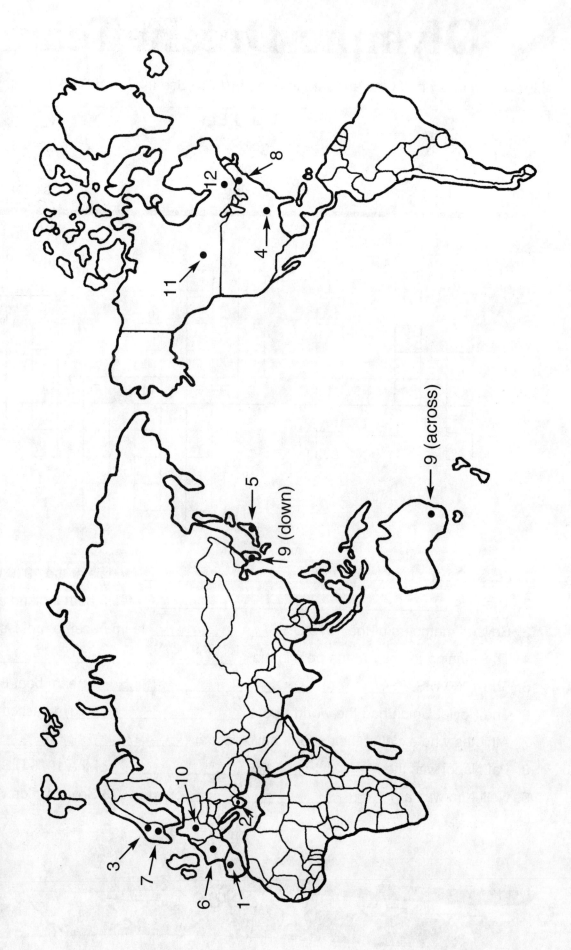

Answer Key

Page 4

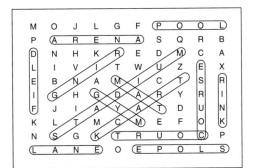

Page 7

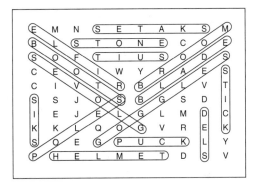

Page 5

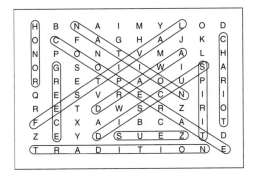

Page 8

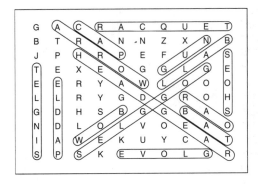

Page 6

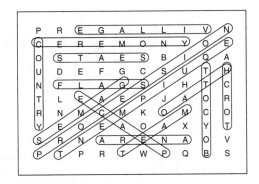

Page 9

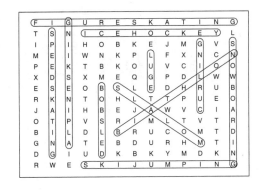

Answer Key *(cont.)*

Page 10

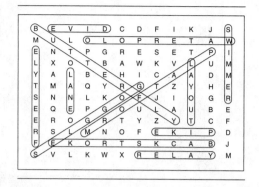

Page 13

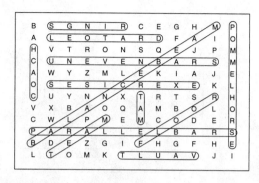

Page 11

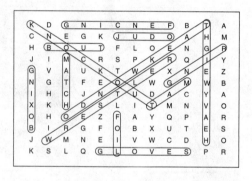

Page 14

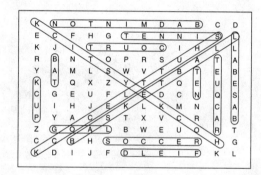

Page 12

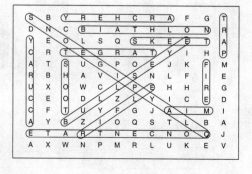

Page 15

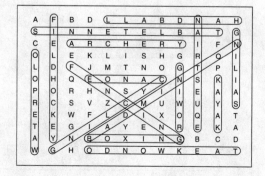

Answer Key *(cont.)*

Page 16

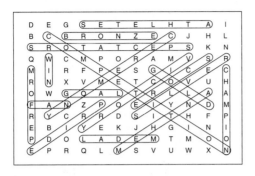

Page 19

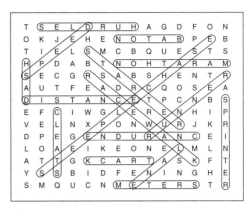

Page 17

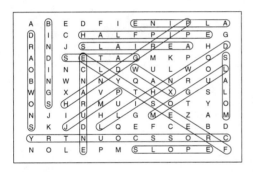

Page 20

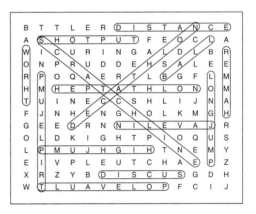

Page 18

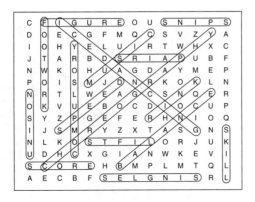

Page 21

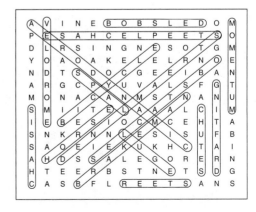

Answer Key *(cont.)*

Page 22

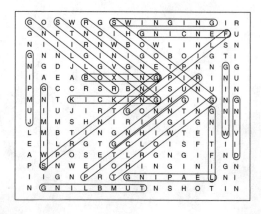

Page 25

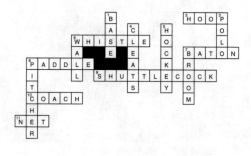

Page 23

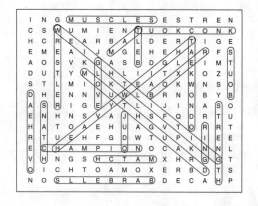

Page 26

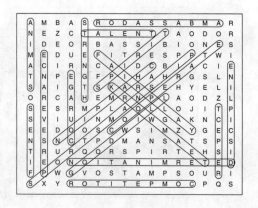

Page 24

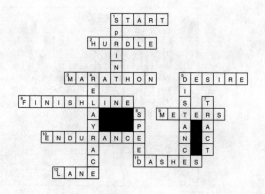

Page 27

Answer Key *(cont.)*

Page 28

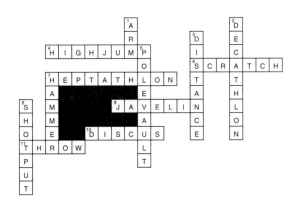

Page 31

Page 29

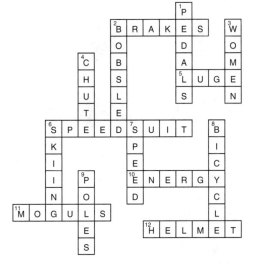

Page 32

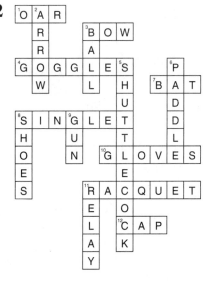

Page 30

Page 33

Answer Key *(cont.)*

Page 34

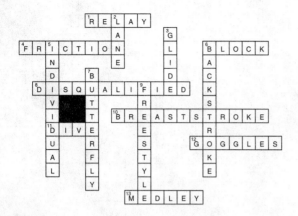

Page 37

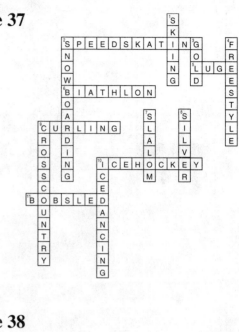

Page 35

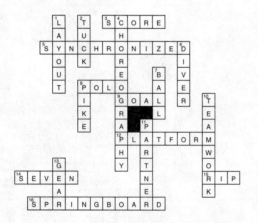

Page 38

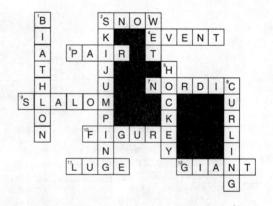

Page 36

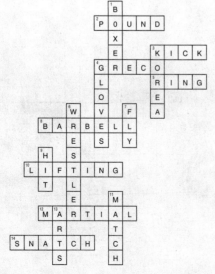

Page 39

Answer Key *(cont.)*

Page 40

Page 43

Page 41

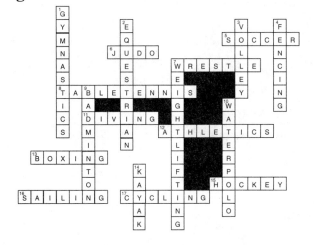

Page 44

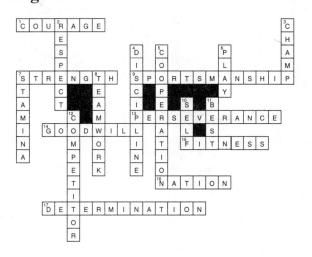

Page 42

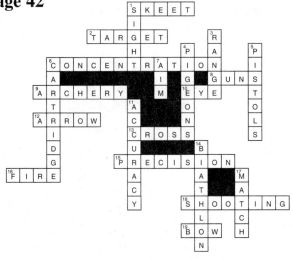

Page 45

Answer Key *(cont.)*

Page 46

Page 47

Page 48

1. Berlin
2. Olympics
3. Los Angeles
4. Medals

Page 49

1. Bonnie Blair
2. Eric Heiden
3. Australia
4. Mexico
5. United States
6. Canada
7. South Korea
8. Norway
9. Japan
10. Carl Lewis
11. Mary Lou Retton
12. Janet Evans
13. Matt Biondi
14. Bruce Jenner
15. Greg Louganis

Bonus: Afghanistan

Page 50

1. Olympia
2. citizens
3. athletes
4. foot
5. gods
6. five
7. chariot
8. horse
9. pentathlon
10. wrestling
11. rod
12. excluded

Page 51

1. puck
2. five
3. oar
4. paddle
5. glove
6. hurdle
7. run
8. rink
9. ten
10. round
11. stick
12. hoop
13. lie
14. blade
15. throw
16. court
17. fall
18. Nordic
19. foot
20. decathlon

Answer Key *(cont.)*

Page 52

1. C
2. F
3. G
4. J
5. O
6. D
7. I
8. H
9. E
10. Q
11. A
12. P
13. B
14. M
15. K
16. N
17. L

Page 53

1. 776 B.C.
2. 200 meters
3. 70,000
4. 4
5. 40-foot
6. 1 month
7. 13
8. 12
9. 3, 5
10. 12

Page 56

The site of the first modern Olympic Games: Athens, Greece

Page 57

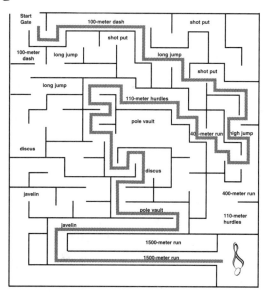

Page 58

Students will supply the names of Olympic athletes who could be described by the following personalized license plates:

1. speed skater
2. great boxer
3. dream team (U.S. basketball player)
4. figure skater
5. #1 diver
6. soccer great
7. 7 gold medals in 1972 (Mark Spitz)
8. possibilities include: any gold-medal winning decathlete; or Nadia Comaneci, who scored perfect 10s to win a gold medal.

Page 59

1. Owens
2. Lewis
3. Yamaguchi
4. Malone
5. Spitz
6. Lipinski
7. Capriati
8. Jansen
9. Strug

Answer Key *(cont.)*

Page 60

1. bow, arrows, target
2. ball, bat, glove
3. tennis, volleyball
4. discus, javelin, shotput
5. parallel bars, balance beam
6. sailing, canoeing
7. fencing, riding, shooting, running, swimming

Page 61

1. run
2. miss
3. hot
4. walk
5. silver
6. water
7. puck
8. athlete
9. grass
10. kick
11. sled
12. ski jump
13. field hockey
14. tens

Page 62

1. United States
2. Ethiopia
3. diving
4. gold
5. archery
6. horse
7. soccer
8. ring
9. third place
10. shoot
11. track
12. racquet
13. uneven bars
14. pentathlon

Page 63

1. baseball, baseball mitt
2. hockey stick
3. ski poles
4. uneven bars, parallel bars
5. boxing gloves
6. tennis racquet

Page 64

1. opening ceremony
2. yellow, green, and red

Page 65

1. archery
2. basketball
3. baseball
4. tennis
5. track and field
6. hockey
7. fencing
8. swimming
9. skiing
10. skating
11. sledding
12. gymnastics

Page 66

Answers will vary.

Page 67

1. U.S. Female Wins Skating Gold—Tara Lipinski
2. Berlin Honors U.S. Track Star—Jesse Owens
3. U.S. Man Youngest Decathlon Winner—Bob Mathias
4. U.S. Swimmer Takes Seven Golds—Mark Spitz
5. Winning Gymnast Injures Ankle—Keri Strug

Page 68

1. Paavo Nurmi
2. Nadia Comaneci
3. Sonja Henie
4. Dawn Fraser
5. Anton Sailer

Page 69

1. gold
2. hockey
3. boxing
4. world
5. basketball
6. women's
7. talent
8. coach
9. gymnast